Edward Harold Browne, W lliam Page Wood Hatherley

A Speech not spoken : being a letter to the Right Hon. the

Lord Hatherley,

Lord High Chancellor of England, on the Irish Church Bill

Edward Harold Browne, William Page Wood Hatherley

A Speech not spoken : being a letter to the Right Hon. the Lord Hatherley,
Lord High Chancellor of England, on the Irish Church Bill

ISBN/EAN: 9783744789967

Printed in Europe, USA, Canada, Australia, Japan

Cover: Foto ©Lupo / pixelio.de

More available books at **www.hansebooks.com**

A SPEECH NOT SPOKEN:

BEING

A LETTER

TO THE

RIGHT HON. THE LORD HATHERLEY,

LORD HIGH CHANCELLOR OF ENGLAND,

ON

THE IRISH CHURCH BILL.

BY

EDWARD HAROLD

BISHOP OF ELY.

LONDON:

LONGMANS, GREEN, AND CO.

1869.

LONDON: PRINTED BY
SPOTTISWOODE AND CO., NEW-STREET SQUARE
AND PARLIAMENT STREET

LETTER.

MY DEAR LORD,

The Irish Church Bill must soon come on in the House of Lords. A great many noble Lords, and, still more probably, a great many Right Reverend Prelates, will desire to address the House. Few perhaps, of the Bishops especially, will like to give a silent vote. As there are three Archbishops, three Irish Bishops, and many others who from age, station, high intellect, or commanding eloquence will have a just claim to be listened to, some of us must be content to be hearers only. Will you, therefore, bear with me if I, as one of those, ask you to let me write to you some things which I would willingly say to somebody? Your Lordship is Chairman of that august assembly, in which, by the providence of God and the good pleasure of my sovereign, I have the honour to hold a seat. I have experienced many times your courteous, and much more than courteous, kindness. I know you to be superior to mere party considerations, and I verily believe that you hold your high office as a trust from above, and will act in it as having an account to give to a tribunal as unlike as it is superior to human opinion or popular applause. The newspapers tell us often enough that a British Parliament never condescends to arguments based on the principles of religion, and especially of the Christian religion. I cannot say that that has been my experience of the House of Lords. It is, however, obvious that some things which might be said in Church would not sound well in Parliament. And, perhaps, as a Christian Bishop dealing with a great religious question, I may write to one whose whole life has testified to his deep value for religious truth, more freely and more fully than I might speak to any general assembly, how much soever to be honoured and esteemed.

Let me say then, my Lord, that I feel most deeply the difficulty of the question with which the present Cabinet has had to deal. I am fully alive to the anomaly of a Church containing but 700,000 worshippers being treated as the Church of a people numbering nearly 6,000,000 souls. I think too, that the proposals of the late Commission would not satisfy either the people of Ireland or the clergy of Ireland; that, if acted on, they would weaken the Church, and yet would not silence its enemies. I have no question that that eminent statesman, who is specially responsible for the pending Bill, has brought it forward in a spirit of anxious desire to remedy a grievance, to conciliate a nation, and to do even-handed justice to all. Especially I am sensible of the grievous wrongs which for centuries have been suffered by Ireland, for which in various ways England is responsible, for which England ought to feel shame and penitence, and for the righting of which England for herself ought to spare no pains, no expense, and no suffering.

And in this, my Lord, it is that the real difficulty is seated. No man, or body of men, can do wrong without being in danger of doing further and, very likely, greater wrong. Herod's rash oath could not be escaped from but by murder or by perjury. The way in which Ireland has been dealt with, both in religion and politics, from the time of Henry II. to the time of George III., has made it impossible to redress her grievances without doing mischief on the one side or the other. And, of course, the reality of past grievances will ever give a colour of truth to fictitious grievances, whether in the minds of the people or in the mouths of their misleaders.

One natural argument against the Irish Church is, that it is a badge of conquest. It may be so ; but what is not? The Court in Dublin, the Lord-Lieutenant, the military, the police, the gentry bearing Norman and Saxon names—above all, the tenure of the land, are as much badges of conquest, and some of them much more offensive to the people, than the Church establishment. And then, again, what was the conquest? It certainly was no conquest of a Roman Catholic by a Protestant people ; nor even was it the conquest of Ireland by England. As a matter of fact, the real conquerors of Ireland were equally the conquerors of England. England was conquered, and her customs, civil and religious, were changed by Norman invaders. Ireland was conquered only a century after by the same race—a race then dominant in England, but not then English ; for the Normans and Saxons did not cohere and become one nation till a later reign than that of Henry II. And as for the religious question, it was the Pope himself, Adrian IV., who gave over Ireland to those same Norman conquerors. Ireland was not submissive enough to his authority, and so the

Roman Patriarch delivered her into the hands of the king of England, on condition that he should levy Peter's pence from her children, and in all ways insist on her subjection to Rome. In truth, therefore, Roman Catholic Ireland was never conquered by Protestant England; but Ireland—then most imperfectly, if at all, Romanised—was conquered by the Norman conquerors of England at the instigation of the Sovereign Pontiff.

I do not deny, but rather insist, that the wrong thus begun was continued and perpetuated by the English Government through successive generations. It is hard to tell when, and by whom, the worst was done. The Irish people were ever restless under the yoke imposed on them, and so ever provoking the severity of their governors. Whether we look at the ages, from the conquest to the Reformation, when England was at least as Romish as Ireland, or at the great reforming monarchs Henry VIII. and Elizabeth, or at the great Puritan Protector, it is difficult to say when and by whom the greatest injury was done to the property, the religion, and the lives of Irish people. The history is one shifting scene of injustice and oppression, culminating in that which has become a proverb, 'the curse of Cromwell.' But the Church of Ireland was not the doer of all this. It was the rulers of England that did it, and they did it as much to the Church, both before and since the Reformation, as they did it to the people.

The Normans were not the first to introduce an alien clergy and an alien episcopate into Ireland, for the Danes (also Northmen) had already done so in the 11th century; but the Normans riveted the chain both of political and spiritual supremacy on the neck of the

Irish people, made their Church one with the English Church, and, though they certainly brought improvements into its system, they effectually reduced it into bondage both to England and to Rome. Moreover, never was there such disaffection to the Government or such a war of races as from the year of the conquest, 1171, to the time of the Reformation, nearly four centuries after; and never had the Irish greater reason to complain of their rulers, whether in Church or in State. And complain they did. In 1318 the Irish complained to the Pope, whose predecessor had handed them over to the power of Henry II. They complained of the cruelty of the English Government, and especially of the oppression of the Church of Ireland by her English ecclesiastical rulers; but so far were they from obtaining redress that in 1367 the famous Statute of Kilkenny was made by English bishops, nobles, and members of parliament, which forbade Irishmen to use their own language among Englishmen, and forbade Irishmen to be received into religious houses or instituted to benefices among the English in Ireland.

Let it be remembered, then, that English oppression of Ireland, the oppression of the Irish by the English Church, was no product of the Reformation—was not simply an oppression of Roman Catholics by Protestants. It actually commenced with the introduction of Romanism into Ireland; for from the time of St. Patrick, A.D. 440, to the conquest by Henry II., A.D. 1171, a period of 731 years, the Church of Ireland had not been subject to the See of Rome; but from 1171 to 1536, a period of 365 years, it was subjected to Rome by the Norman conquerors both of England and of Ireland, and never was it more oppressed, more restless, more dissatisfied than during these 365 years.

Let us pass to the Reformation. Did the Irish Church accept the Reformation? This is a question which people will solve in different ways. The Irish bishops, with the exception of two, remained in their sees, and the great body of the clergy retained their benefices. These bishops and clergy accepted—some with a good, others with a bad will—those changes of doctrine and discipline commonly called the Reformation. Much the same took place in England, and very likely the Reformation would have taken as deep a root in Ireland as it did in England but for the continuance by the English Government of the miserable policy which was begun in the time of the Roman supremacy. Again the Irish language was proscribed; the prayers were not to be said in Irish, but in English; or if the minister did not know English, still not in Irish, but in Latin.

The more wise and pious among the prelates wished to give the people the Irish Scriptures, but the authorities of the State forbade their circulation: they wished to discourage the Irish language altogether, and so they would not let the Irish be taught even the faith of Christ in the tongue of their fathers and their homes. The Court of Rome, which had never succoured Ireland so long as England was keeping Ireland subject to the Pope, now, in the eleventh year of Elizabeth, sent over an alien episcopate and an alien clergy to Ireland, and, with true wisdom, encouraged what England had discouraged—the teaching of the people in their native tongue. Thus the great body of the peasantry were drawn off from the Church—the Church planted by St. Patrick, subjected for a time (361 years) to Rome, and reformed in the reigns of Henry and Elizabeth. A Church which was the true Church of the nation was prevented by the civil power in England from offering to its people the pure water of life in all its freshness; and so they naturally sought it from other, though it may be more corrupted sources.

More or less the same policy went on: and not only were the people denied the use of their own language in Christian worship, but the high places of the Church were filled from time to time with ecclesiastics who would not have been tolerated in like positions in England. It is not very long since ministers of generally high character and honour could treat the bishoprics and archbishoprics of Ireland as mere shelves on which to lay political partizans and personal friends.

I have said that the Church of Ireland is still the same Church that it was from the time of St. Patrick to the time of the conquest under Henry II., and, again, from that time to the Reformation. Your Lordship knows very well, that from the earliest ages of the faith the continuity of a Church has always been esteemed to depend on the continuity of its episcopate. The fathers of the primitive Church carefully traced the descent of their bishops from the apostles on this very principle. As a race or nation is esteemed to be the same if it be handed down by successive generations from father to son; so the Christian Church, from the very beginning, always held that bishops, being the fathers of the Church, handed down the race by successive generations. The Irish Church, therefore, having its episcopate unchanged, has retained its ecclesiastical identity. One body of bishops was not displaced at the Reformation and another put in its room. Roman Catholics assert, however, that if unity of descent was not, still unity of faith and doctrine was broken. If it be meant that every change in the doctrinal tenets of a Church destroys its identity, then is there no Church which has not been destroyed. The mediæval Church was so different from the primitive Church in many of its tenets and practices, that, if unity in minute points be indispensable, no Church can maintain its historical identity. But I fearlessly assert that almost all Churches have held fast those great charters, those main principles of ecclesiastical life, which are essential to the being and the true succession of a Church. Most certainly, neither the Irish nor the English Church, from the first foundation to the present day, have ever let go the creeds of Catholic Christendom, the belief in the great cardinal doctrines of the Trinity, the Incarnation, the Atoning Sacrifice, the Resurrection, the General Judgment, the Life Eternal; nor have they ever given up the apostolic ordination of their clergy, the use of the great sacraments instituted by Christ, nor, indeed, any single ordinance traceable to the first ages of the faith. The English Constitution has gone through changes a thousand times greater than the English Church has gone through, and yet we cling to it as our great inheritance, linking us on to past ages of wisdom and heroism, and which we hope, or once hoped, we might hand down to our children's children. The first Reform Bill altered the constitution of the nation as much as, and the Revolution altered it much more than, the Reformation altered the constitution of the National Church. If, notwithstanding the Revolution, we do not doubt the continued identity of the nation, we have no reason, because of the Reformation, to doubt the identity of the Church.

For my present argument, however, I have no need to press either the succession of the bishops, the continuity of doctrine, or even the identity of the Church. I am quite willing to acknowledge that the body of the Irish people never embraced the Reformation. The efforts of their rulers to force it upon them, and the means adopted for that purpose, such as proscribing their language and sending to them strange teachers with English tongues, effectually prevented them from accepting it. The Crown exercised its supremacy in a manner which we could not tolerate at present. What is now called the Royal Supremacy is an expression of the principle that priests are not to lord it over God's heritage, but that the laity have a right to a controlling power, so as not to be forced to receive forms of teaching or of worship from which their consciences revolt. Therefore the highest authority in a nation is also invested with the highest authority in a national church. But in Tudor times the Crown overrode both clergy and laity. When Edward and Elizabeth reigned all were required to accept the Reformation, and when Mary reigned all were required to reject it.

The principle, however, on which the upholding by the governing power of the Reformation in Ireland has been and still may be fairly defended, is this. From the time of the conquest the two nations, England and Ireland, had become one nation, the two Churches of England and Ireland had become one Church. When the Reformation came, though only a remnant accepted it on one side of the Channel, yet a large majority accepted it on the other side of the Channel: hence a clear majority of the whole nation and a clear majority of the whole Church accepted it. There was no thought of disintegrating either the nation or the Church. Hence it was obvious that the minority must yield to the majority, though unfortunately the great body of the dissentients were separated from the great body of the conformists by seventy miles of sea.

Theoretically I cannot see that this principle breaks down at all; and it explains the apparent anomaly of Scotland having adopted the Reformation very differently from England and Ireland. In the 16th century England and Ireland were one; England and Ireland had but one Church, and it was reformed as one undivided whole. But in the same 16th century England and Scotland were two; and when Scotland reformed its Church, it had no need to ask leave of England and of the English Church, for it was an independent, separate State, with an independent, distinct Church; and when, in the 17th century, the Crowns of England and Scotland were united, the Reformation had already been effected in England and Ireland in one way, and in Scotland in another way. The two therefore independent nations (England and Scotland) coalesced, each determining to keep its own forms of faith and worship, notwithstanding their disagreement, the one from the other. The efforts of the Stuart sovereigns to introduce the principles of the English Church into Scotland were not unnaturally resisted by the Scottish people. Such an introduction was illegal and illogical; for it was not, as in the case of Ireland, making the will of the minority bend to the will of the majority, but it was giving a retrospective force to the union, acting as though the union had existed before the Reformation begun.

Practically, however, the difficulty is this. For seven hundred years England has considered Ireland as one with itself, and has tried to make it more and more so. But in this, the eighth century from the conquest, we are becoming painfully alive to the fact, that the union has been maintained by force, not by affection ; that the two races have not amalgamated ; that though the Celt and the Saxon live close together, they do not, like brethren, live together in unity ; that even on the Irish soil itself there has been no coalescing, as there soon was of the Norman with the Saxon in England, and that the Irishman, who does not love the Anglo-Irishman, too often actually hates the true Englishman. Hence, of late, statesmen begin to legislate as though Ireland were not one people with England, and as though the Church of Ireland were distinct from the Church of England. This, I suppose, is the logical principle of disestablishing the Irish Church whilst leaving the English Church established. It is no longer conceded that England and Ireland are one in Church and State, having one voice—viz., the voice of their united majority. They are now looked on as two ; and then it is obviously hard that the 700,000 Anglicans should be the spokesmen for, and utter the voice of the whole 6,000,000 inhabitants of Ireland. It is held that a foreign pressure—viz., the pressure of the English Government—forced the Reformation on the Irish Church and the Irish people, and that they ought now in fairness to be withdrawn.

I will not now discuss the justice or the injustice of this conclusion. Let us admit it for the sake of argument, and we then have new premises for a further argument. The conclusion to which these new premises have led the Government is, that the Church, thus said to have been reformed by compulsion, ought now to be disestablished, disendowed, and turned out empty-handed on the world.

I confess I cannot see the soundness of the reasoning. The Church of Ireland was certainly, from the time of St. Patrick to the time of the Reformation, the recognised, protected, honoured, endowed Church of the nation. Say the Reformation was forced upon it against its own convictions and against the convictions of the people of the land. Where lay the fault? Not surely with the oppressed Church, but with the oppressing English nation. A change in forms of worship and in certain articles of faith was forced upon the Church— the Church was compelled (according to the theory) to accept the change; it was bidden to work as a police-force in the land—to hold it like a garrison for the English nation. It might have done so far more effec- tually if it had been left a little freer; but because it has done as the English nation ordered it to do—only somewhat better and in a more Christian spirit than the wording of its orders prescribed—therefore it is to be suddenly dispossessed, and its property to be taken from it, by that very power whose intentions it is said to have carried out only too faithfully. Can this be a logical conclusion, or strict justice either to the Church or to the people of Ireland? Ireland has within it a machinery, erected in it from the earliest times, cal- culated, if rightly worked, to confer upon it the greatest blessings which a people can have—viz., re- ligion and civilisation; but the wheels, and ropes, and pulleys have been clogged, tied up, and knotted by an external and a hostile pressure; therefore break the wheels, and cut the pulleys, and destroy this mechanism which a thousand years have been building up, and then recommend the people to set to work again and try if they cannot weave a new web for themselves, which, perhaps, another besom of destruction will sweep away hereafter.

I submit that the true logical conclusion from the premises (if correct) would be, not to destroy the machinery, but to remove the pressure. If we acknowledge the Irish people and the Irish Church to be distinct and separate from the English, then it is but reasonable to say: The English people have been exercising the tyranny of a numerical majority over the Irish people; by weight of that majority they have forced the Reformation on a Church which did not want the Reformation. We have now awoke to a sense of our iniquity—we remove the force, we leave you to your freedom; if the Church has been too much reformed by us, it is quite competent to you to institute a counter-reformation—only leave the present occupants, bishops and curates, in possession of their sees and their cures for life; but, if it be the will of the people, let those sees and cures at their avoidance pass in due succession to bishops and priests who will subscribe to the Council of Trent, instead of passing to those who subscribe the Thirty-Nine Articles.

There is another possible course. I have reasoned on the assumption (which I hold to be true) that the present Irish Church, like the English branch of the same Church, has, though reformed, yet retained the succession of bishops from St. Patrick to this day. I believe in its continuity of life, and that the present Anglo-Irish Church is still the true Catholic Church of Ireland. But some have argued that the true succession is not in the Anglo-Irish Church, but in the Roman Church in Ireland; that the Church of the Reformation did not succeed lineally and by regular descent from the mediæval Church, but that the mediæval bishops perpetuated a true succession in the line of the Roman Catholic hierarchy. As this is an antiquarian or historical question which, it is said, statesmen do not like to hear of, I am not proposing to enter into it. I will merely again, for argument's sake, admit it as premiss for another inference. If this be true, then the English Government, at the time of the Reformation, must be convicted of still greater tyranny than on the other hypothesis. If the English Government, against the will of the people, erected a new Church, and, in order to endow it, robbed the old Church; and if the English Government has now come to its senses, and is satisfied that this was an act of robbery, spoliation, and wrong; then most plainly the course of justice is—not that it should put the plundered money quietly in its own pocket, for its own purposes, but—making the best compensation it can to the body which was its dupe, its tool, or its accomplice—to restore the bulk of the property to the plundered, spoliated Church.

In that case, the logical conclusion must be, that, when the present occupants of sees and benefices vacate, each vacant living and see should be handed over to the present Roman Catholic Church.

Now, my Lord, I have all my life been a warm supporter of the great principles of the English Reformation. Whether they were always carried out rightly is another point, but the principles I believe to have been essentially true. I am not therefore **very** likely to desire to see the Roman Church established and endowed and honoured in the heart of the empire. Still, I maintain, that on logical grounds, and grounds of strict justice, if we assume the principles now generally insisted on, viz., either (1) that the Church of Ireland was unjustly compelled to accept the Reformation, or (2) that the present Roman Catholic Church is the true and ancient Church of the land, retaining the ancient succession both of clergy and of doctrine; then the inference must be from the first of the two principles (1) to give free scope to the Irish people to re-reform their Church, to re-introduce Romish doctrines and practices; or, from the latter of the two principles (2), to strip the Reformed Church of the revenues which by this hypothesis were never lawfully hers, and to give them over to the Roman Church. No case has been made out for taking away the revenues altogether and secularising them, or confiscating them to the State; for in either alternative the State was (1) the oppressor, or (2) the robber; in one case the Church was oppressed and injured, in the other the Roman Church was robbed and ought to be righted, whilst the Protestant Church was at worst the receiver of stolen goods from the robber State.

I see no reply to this, but either that in the teeth of English Protestantism such strict justice cannot be done, or that the evil of endowing Romanism is greater than that of robbing the Church of God. Would you not rather say, *Fiat justitia, ruat cœlum?* However, I am not advocating this. I am merely pointing out, that, if we are to have what is acknowledged to be a great revolution, but a revolution rendered imperative in order to set right an intolerable wrong, then we ought to set it right in the right way, and not, for the sake of setting it right, to do another wrong—after all leaving it very doubtful whether any real right has been done at all. If a case were brought before the Court of Chancery in which one party was in possession of property, whilst another party alleged that property to have been fraudulently taken from him, and if the fraud were proved against the actual possessor, I do not think your Lordship's judgment would be: 'The property clearly belongs to the claimant, not to the actual possessor; the actual possessor must therefore, in justice, give it up : but as the claimant has been for a very long time deprived of it, and so cannot reasonably want it, and as he is a suspicious character, and may perhaps make a bad use of it, he therefore shall not succeed to the possession of it. Rather let it go to the skilful lawyer who obtained it for his own client, the present occupant, because he is in great need of it, has a large family and many clamorous dependents, and because the High Court of Chancery very properly protects the interests of all branches of the law.'

My Lord, I repeat that it would be painful to me, as a Bishop of the English Church, to see in the sister island a branch of the Roman Church established, as it is called, and in union with the Government of this country : but as I have endeavoured to show that this would be more logical and more equitable than the utter disestablishment and disendowment of the Church, so do I believe that in the end it would prove less dangerous to that which you and I both most value in the faith, and also to the peace and union of the two

countries. I hope I may be mistaken ; but to me it
seems inevitable that the sudden disestablishment of
the Irish Church will give a much speedier and more
certain supremacy to the Church of Rome than any
other conceivable measure. Of course, it is said that
the lay members of the Anglican Church in Ireland
have the great wealth of the country in their hands ;
that they are, therefore, well able to maintain their
own Church ; and that the Church set free will act
more freely, and so effect more good. I confess that,
if we had to choose between disestablished and disendowed freedom and the kind of bondage once, and
not long since, imposed on the Irish Church, it would
be far better to have freedom and poverty than honour
and wealth with the mouth stopped and the hands tied.
But the old system of forbidding the Irish language
and the like can never come again. And then, on the
other hand, it seems impossible that the Irish Church
with its present prospects can make head against the
Roman Church. First, for the money question. Rich
landlords, if such they be, many of them absentees, will
never support a Church and a clergy. A man who
possessed all the land in a parish, would be a prodigy of
Christian liberality (as times go) if he were to provide
even £300 a year for the income of the clergyman and
the support of the fabric and services of the Church.
How many such are to be found in Ireland or in England ?
I fear we must say, that, with a few brilliant exceptions,
the rich laity in our Church have never yet learned to
give. It is most true, as the Bishop of Ossory has shown,
that a Church which is to depend on voluntary contri-
butions must seek them from its many poor, not from
its few rich. The £10 or £50 annual donations of

the rich squire will tell but little compared with the weekly pence and sixpences of the pious poor. A Church, therefore, which looks to its landowners for support has a broken reed to rest on.

And, once more, though we are told that the Irish Church will now be set free, and will then be able to act more independently, and so more successfully, yet we must remember, that it has for centuries been denied all free action and even free speech. It will be like a man for years fettered and manacled and imprisoned, suddenly let loose and bid to work for his living, to exercise his calling, and to defend himself against his enemies. The Church of Ireland probably has had less of organic and corporate life than any Church or sect in Christendom. It will be confronted with the most perfect organization ever devised by man. What can be its prospects? A bright picture might no doubt be drawn of a Christian country in which every little village had its own church, its own pastor, its own internal organization, needing but little intercourse with other parishes or other pastors, and all the happier for its quiet, uneventful, unambitious life. All this is conceivable in the simplest conditions of rural life, and looks very pleasant upon paper, even with the possibility that such 'sweet Auburns' might pass into 'Sleepy Hollows.' But in the din and strife and struggle of life and thought in Christendom now, such scenes can be but rare indeed. And all experience shows that if a Church or a sect is to maintain its existence and to do its work, it must, on the principle of natural selection, either be a great secret society, interpenetrating all Christendom, such as the Church of Rome, or it must openly enlist and consolidate its clergy and its laity together in one organic body, to counsel and work and give for the great end and aim which then all will have in view. This is exactly what the English Church has not done, and what the Irish Church has done still less. It has been no fault of its own that it has not done so. The power which at one time forbade it to speak to its own people in their own tongue, has even to this day forbidden it to meet in Convocation, or to assume any true internal organization. It has hitherto, no doubt, had a machinery which has supplied the want and evaded the necessity for such internal organization, viz., the civil machinery of parishes, and vestries, and church-rates, and tithe-rent charges, and churchwardens, and corporations sole, and ecclesiastical courts. But the instant you take away its nationality, organization and corporate life and corporate action will all be gone. And what hope is there that this unorganized, cramped, confined body—cramped by those who have professed to protect it—with no support but that of the un-giving rich, shall in a fair field hold its own against the highly-organized, powerful, not only free but long-dominant Church, which (let us not grudge it its well-merited honour) has largely enlisted the affections of the poor? We must remember, too, that the Roman Catholic priesthood have a resource which no Reformed clergy can have. The doctrine of purgatory is a boundless mine of wealth. I am not going to make the popular charges against the Roman clergy of imposing on the credulity of the people for the sake of their own interests. No doubt the Irish priest believes the doctrine of purgatory and the efficacy of masses for the dead, as much as the Irish peasant to whom he teaches them. This does not alter the fact that a man who believes that his mother is in purgatory, and that money given in masses can relieve and abridge her sufferings, will give all he can to the Church for saying those masses.

To all human appearance, therefore, the setting free from State control and from ancient endowment of the Church of Ireland in its present condition must give an easy victory and an undivided empire to the Church of Rome. And I believe that it would be safer at once to establish that Church, and install it in all the privileges of the national Church of Ireland, than thus to let it become national in spite of you. A national Church must always be amenable, more or less, to national law. The national Churches of France and Austria, and even of Spain and Italy, have always been in some measure restrained by their nationality. But the Roman Church in Ireland, if it does thoroughly overrun and subjugate the whole island, will be amenable only to a tribunal in Italy, and the sovereignty of the Supreme Pontiff will be absolute and unlimited.

There are then three theories, according to which it seems reasonable that the country should judge and act. *The first* is, that England and Ireland have been one people for many centuries, and their Church one ; that therefore the Reformation, carried by a majority of the whole people, was a legitimate and constitutional proceeding. If we admit this, the Irish Church has a just claim to its present position and its present revenues ; and it has inherited both from the fifth century to this day. *The second* is, that England and Ireland being two distinct peoples, the Reformation was unjustly forced upon the Irish Church by its English rulers. If this be true, the conclusion surely is, that the Irish people should be allowed now to legislate for themselves and for their own Church, and, if they see fit, duly regarding present interests, to re-reform their Church. *The third* is, that the Roman Church was robbed at the Reformation in order to establish and endow the Protestant Church. This indeed is the most untenable of all, and, as a matter of history, is simply false. But, if it were true, the logical and equitable conclusion would be, not to confiscate the revenues, but to restore them to their original owners. To no one of these three hypotheses —and I cannot see a fourth—does the present plan of disestablishment and disendowment seem a reasonable consequence. I believe the nation has determined on it : and, if so, neither the Church nor the House of Lords can resist it. I acknowledge the great embarrassment which a Cabinet must feel in having to legislate for Ireland in the present crisis; I acknowledge the great ability with which the scheme of disestablishment has been evolved; I have already acknowledged the conscientious honesty as well as the consummate skill of him who has framed it. I wish I could see the faintest hope that it would secure the peace, the happiness, or the piety of the people for whose benefit it is designed.

And now, may I go on to say a few words on a more general question—the question, I mean, of Established Churches, or of the union of Church and State ? It is acknowledged that in the present day many religious men and devoted Churchmen are, at least, growing cool in their zeal for such establishments ; some are even looking anxiously for the time when the

Church shall be set free from 'the galling fetters of the State.' I respect the sentiment, but I cannot share in it.

Your Lordship, in hours stolen from the heavy labours of your judicial offices, has studied and written concerning the continuity of Holy Scripture. May I ask you whether you have not observed that two great leading thoughts pervade it all? One of these is the great but most mysterious doctrine of Sacrifice; the other is the perpetual acknowledgment, the systematic tracing, from Genesis to the Apocalypse, of the great invisible Theocracy. In the family of Seth, of Shem, of Abraham, of Jacob—through the whole history of Judah and Israel—the Old Testament traces the stream of the Theocratic government, and the fortunes of the Theocratic race. The New Testament is the expansion of the Theocracy in Israel into the Kingdom of God among all the nations of the earth. John the Baptist preached the Kingdom of God as near at hand (Matt. iii. 2, &c.). Jesus Christ preached the Kingdom of God (Matt. iv. 17; x. 7; Luke iv. 43; viii. 1; Acts i. 3, &c.). He commissioned His disciples and all that would follow Him to preach the Kingdom of God (Luke ix. 2, 60, &c. &c.). The apostles, after His resurrection, went about preaching the Kingdom of God (Acts viii. 12; xix. 8; xx. 25; xxviii. 23, 31, &c.). The most marked change introduced into the world by the Gospel itself was the taking of the Kingdom from the Jewish people, who had shown themselves unfit for it, and the setting up the same Kingdom among the whole human race. The apostolic commission was to teach all nations, and to admit them by baptism as subjects of that Kingdom which God had set up in Christ.

Without doubt, at first the Christian Theocracy had to struggle, in depression and apparent defeat, against another kingdom, as the Theocracy had done before with the patriarchs in Palestine and with the Israelites in Egypt. But when the emperor of the world and the various earthly kingdoms embraced the faith, accepted the Church, and submitted to the reign of the Saviour, the Christians of old recognised in that event an accomplishment (partial, it may be, but real) of the prophecies that kings should be the nursing fathers, and queens the nursing mothers, of the Church (Isai. xlix. 23); in the failure of heathen before Christian nations, they read the truth of those words—'the nation and the kingdom which will not serve thee' (the Theocracy) 'shall perish' (Isa. lx. 12); in the wide and rapid diffusion of the Theocracy, and the honour, support, and allegiance accorded to it by the nations, they hailed the fulfilment of the Apocalyptic vision, 'the kingdoms of this world are become the kingdoms of our God and of His Christ' (Rev. xi. 15).

My Lord, I have no doubt that they were right. There may be—probably there will be—a still higher accomplishment of all these prophecies; but I am confident that the great Christian thinkers of old—and I doubt if any greater thinkers ever wrote their thoughts —were right in their belief that the Kingdom of God had come; that the God of Heaven had set up a Kingdom never to be destroyed; that He had anointed His King upon His holy hill of Zion; that He had ordained that all nations, kingdoms, and languages should serve Him; that there was therefore in this world a true *Civitas Dei*—a true reign of Christ—and that the outward organization of it was the universal Church.

So strongly was this the primitive belief, that this accepted reign of Christ in the civilised and then known world was identified with the thousand years in which it is said by St. John that the saints should reign on earth; and at the end of the tenth century, it being thought that this millennium was literally a thousand years and no more, and that it was, therefore, then coming to an end, men made their wills and devised their property, beginning legal documents with the words '*Appropinquante jam mundi termino.*' The failure to interpret details of obscure prophecy is no proof that the first ten centuries of Christian men erred in their general acknowledgment of the present Kingdom of Christ, and of the duty and blessing, both of men and of nations, to accept, defend, and honour it.

Now this acceptance of the Theocracy by the nations was what we now call by an unfortunate and, as I think, most inaccurate term—' the establishment of the Church.' Every nation that accepted the Gospel, acknowledged itself bound by the laws of the Gospel, endowed its ministers, protected its worship, and honoured its ordinances. I say, endowed its ministers; I might more correctly say, sanctioned and encouraged their endowment by its people. 'The great mass of Church property is itself the product of charity, the permanent result of the love of souls and the love of God. Cathedrals, hospitals, educational institutions, parochial endowments, are but visible memorials of ancient liberality. The established is, in a great measure, only the voluntary fixed and protected.'* The origin of tithes is, indeed, hidden in great obscurity;

* Archer Butler, *Sermons*, second series, p. 313.

but having been at first, apparently, the offerings of piety, they were at length confirmed and legalized, both by statute and common law.*

---

* Whether tithes were from the first in the English Church or not, is a question not easy to solve. The *Capitula* of Archbishop Theodore, in the seventh century, refer to tithes. The *Excerptions* of Egbright mention them in the middle of the eighth century. In the ninth century we find Ethelwulf, the father of Alfred, making a grant of the tenth of his possessions before going to Rome. In the reigns of Athelstane and Edgar, in the tenth century, we first meet with legislative enactments giving the obligation of law to what appears first to have been a voluntary contribution. In the so-called Canons of Edward the Confessor, tithes are traced to the time of Augustine himself, the Apostle of the Saxons. (See Short, *Hist. of Church of England*, sec. 10; Martineau, *Church Hist. of England*, pp. 121–124, and the authorities there cited and referred to.) Of their early origin in other countries there can be no doubt. They probably were collected in parts of Europe before the end of the fourth century, and some of the Fathers spoke of them as of divine right. (See Bingham, *E. A.* ii. 27, 28.) The Council of Mascon, in the sixth century (can. 5.), speaks of them as of ancient and universal custom. At all events, thus much is certain, that tithes in England can date back their legal obligation for nearly a thousand years. Most probably in England, as elsewhere, they were originally a voluntary gift from the owners of the soil, encouraged and legalized by the authority of the State. Their confiscation, therefore, is surely the taking by the State of that which was given for a special purpose by religious men, and applying it to another and a different purpose. If it be contended that this is not the true history of tithes, but that they were from the first an impost by the State upon the land, and that, therefore, the State can either remit that impost or divert it to other objects, though I cannot admit the soundness of such an hypothesis, it still comes to this: that the nation, in the most solemn manner, has devoted a tenth of its produce to the service of God; that during the whole period of its true national existence it has religiously regarded the obligation so imposed; but that, for reasons of State, it ultimately withdraws the gift. No one doubts the power of a nation over all property and over all national debts; but national honour has hitherto been esteemed as important as personal

Our Anglo-Saxon forefathers not only thus provided a maintenance for the clergy, but they gave them rank and office in the State. From the first, bishops took their place in the Witanagemote, filled posts of highest trust in the land, and, in the court of the shire, the earl or alderman and the bishop sat side by side—the earl declaring the law of the land, which the bishop was to temper by declaring the law of God.* Christianity and the Christian Church were thus interwoven, from the very earliest, into the constitution of the country; and Church and State so became one, from the very time that either Church or State could be said to have had a definite existence in the land. The State supported and honoured the Church; the Church sanctified and, in its turn, supported the State. There was no such thing as the State conscience choosing out for itself what form of Christianity it should teach or commend to its people—no choosing between rival communions; for the truth came to our forefathers, whether undimmed or not by error, at all events undivided by disunion and dissent. They simply accepted Christ and the Church of Christ, and acknowledged themselves His servants, and the subjects of His Kingdom, the invisible, eternal Theocracy.

I am quite prepared to hear that all this was brought about by clerical ambition, and that the clergy, under pretext of establishing the Kingdom of their Great

---

honour, and, in this case, the national Creditor is One whose property in the national wealth is prior and superior to that of the nation itself.

* Edgar's *Laws Ecclesiastical*, can. 7, re-enacted in Cnute's *Laws*. See Johnson's *Canons*, part i, pp. 411, sec. 14. Parker: Oxford.

King, were in truth merely protecting the interests of
their own order and caste. Indeed, we have heard it
said by a voice which always commands attention, that
lords and warriors have done much harm in the world,
but that priests have done much more. I am not going
to deny that priests have sometimes been ambitious, and
that, like other men, they have often fought for self
when they persuaded themselves that they were fighting
for God. But a little knowledge of history and a
little fairness in reading it might teach us that some of
their faults, and many of the evil consequences of their
faults, were rendered almost inevitable by the conditions
of past times. I have elsewhere before quoted a
passage, which seems to me so appropriate and true
that I shall make no apology for quoting it now. It is
from one whose authority as an historian is not less
than that of the right honourable gentleman whose
words I have just referred to, and whose prejudices were
certainly not in favour of bishops, or priests, or ecclesiastical corporations. The late Sir James Stephen
writes ; * 'If it be right to condemn the fiscal tyranny
of the Roman rulers, it can hardly be also right to
condemn those sacerdotal claims and those imperial
concessions by which the range of that tyranny was
narrowed. The Church is arraigned as selfish and
ambitious, because it formed itself into a vast clerical
corporation, living under laws and usages peculiar to
itself, and not acknowledging the jurisdiction of the
temporal tribunals. That the Churchmen of the fourth
century lived beneath a ruthless despotism, no one
attempts to deny. That they opposed to it the only

* *Lectures on the History of France.* By the Right Hon. Sir
James Stephen. Vol. i., pp. 33-37.

barrier by which the imperial tyranny could in that age be arrested in its course, is equally indisputable. . . . . . We may rejoice to know that the early Church was the one great antagonist of the wrongs which were then done upon the earth—that she narrowed the range of fiscal tyranny—that she mitigated the overwhelming poverty of the people—that she promoted the accumulation of capital—that she contributed to the restoration of agriculture—that she balanced and held in check the imperial despotism— that she revived within herself the remembrance and the use of the franchise of popular election—and that the gloomy portraits which have been drawn of her internal and moral state are the mere exaggerations of those who would render the Church responsible for the crimes with which it is her office to contend, and for the miseries which it is her high commission effectually, though gradually, to relieve.' These are the words, not of an ecclesiastic, but of a statesman, and a statesman of the most liberal sentiments both as a politician and as a Churchman. The words would be scarcely less true if used of the bishops and clergy in the reigns of our own Norman Sovereigns. The clergy, no doubt, struggled for their own rights, and perhaps too much against the rights of the Sovereign ; but their own rights were ever exercised to raise the condition of the people, to advance the freedom of the subject, to alleviate the sufferings of the poor. The bishops, quite as much as the temporal barons, with Stephen Langton, Archbishop of Canterbury, as the leader of both, obtained Magna Charta for the nation ; the abbeys and religious houses so provided for the employment and the relief of the peasantry, that no poor-law

was ever needed in England till the Reformation had
stripped the Church of the great bulk of its possessions.*
The necessity, to which Sir J. Stephen alludes, of form-
ing a close corporation of the clergy, led indeed to a very
serious evil. The Christian Church, the Kingdom of
the Saviour, the great Theocracy, embraces every Christian man. But the corporate character of the clergy
led to the confusion between the clergy and the Church.
By degrees the interests of the Church became more
and more identified with the interests of the clergy, and
the consequence was the rivalry and jealousy between
the Pontiff and the Prince.

I have already referred to the Norman Princes as
introducing Norman clergy into the Church. Those
Norman clergy carried their appeals to Rome. So the

---

* The one unpardonable crime of the mediæval clergy was, that
they grew rich. Is it wonderful that they did so, since they alone
cultivated the arts of peace, at a time when all others were devoted
to the arts of war ? Ecclesiastics were then not only ministers of
religion : they taught the young, they tilled the soil, they cultivated
the art of healing, they were the scribes, the lawyers, often the
judges of the land. No one can deny that for the most part they
spent their money nobly. All our cathedrals, and most of our
parish churches, were built by clerical liberality. They founded
schools and colleges, built hospitals, protected the fatherless and the
widow, and were the great almoners of the poor. Probably every
cathedral in England was built by its bishops. Some single portions
of my own cathedral, which were built by single bishops, would,
according to the present value of labour and materials, cost 100,000l.
in building. The first college in Cambridge was founded by a predecessor of my own out of his own revenues. A subsequent Bishop
of Ely founded another college in the same university. These are
but single specimens of what was doing everywhere in England by
the clergy ; and they show that, if they were wealthy, their wealth
was better used than it has ever been by any body of men known
to history.

Church of England and of Ireland became more and more connected with the See of Rome. The subsequent struggles between the Pope and the King, for supremacy, in the reigns of Henry II., and every succeeding reign up to those of Henry VIII. and Elizabeth, are familiar to all. It was this conflict which, more than anything else, led to the Reformation. The distinguished orator referred to just now has told us lately that the principle of the Reformation was that every one should be free to choose his own religion for himself. It is quite possible for a person of the present day, especially for one not belonging to the English Church, so to consider it. But anything less like the principle actually enunciated at the Reformation it is difficult to conceive. I am not concerned with any Reformation except that of our own Church; but the way in which the foreign reformers spoke and acted might prove in very few words that they had no such thoughts. As it is plain that no society could be kept together, much less a Church retain its organization, if every one was free to think and to do whatever was right in his own eyes, and as every reformer, English and Continental, desired to improve and strengthen, but not to subvert the Church, so it is plain that none of them can have desired to refer every practice and opinion to each man's arbitrary choice and judgment.

As to the English Reformation, I think your Lordship will agree with me that the principle of isolated individual action was not once propounded, but that the principles really enunciated were these :—

1. That the Church Catholic, though it had not

ceased to be the true Church of Christ, had yet in lapse of time admitted into it certain corruptions in practice and also in doctrine; that great efforts having been made to obtain a general reformation of these errors by the *whole* Church, and such efforts having signally failed, it remained for the bishops, clergy, and laity of each *national* Church to promote reformation within itself; for that, though external unity and uniformity were earnestly to be desired, yet purity of faith and practice was even yet more necessary.

2. That though 'the Church hath authority in controversies of faith,' yet 'it is not lawful for the Church to ordain anything that is contrary to God's Word written,' and 'besides the same ought not enforce anything to be believed *for necessity of salvation.*' (Art. xx.)

3. That where corruption has come into a Church, either in doctrine or in ceremonial, if there be doubt as to the teaching of Holy Scripture, the faith and practice of the primitive ages are the best guides for reformation: so that the reformers endeavoured to 'come as near as they possibly could to the Church of the Apostles and of the old Catholic bishops and fathers, and to direct, according to their customs and ordinances, not only the doctrine, but also the sacraments and the form of common prayer' (Jewell, *Apology*).

4. That the Church of Christ has no universal king but Christ Himself. He is the Great King in all the earth. He dwells ever in His Church. By the omnipresence of His Deity every corner of His Kingdom, and every subject of that Kingdom, is ever present to Him, and by the pervading power of His Spirit He is

present to every one of them. If He were an absent Sovereign, He might need a vice-gerent; but as He is ever present, vice-royalty is inadmissible. Bishops were, indeed, from the earliest times, named vicars of Christ, *vicarii Christi* ; but they were not such vicars as to intervene between Him and His people, but rather ministers of His Regal Court, and, like the lieutenants or sheriffs of counties, administrators of the various provinces of His extended Empire.*

These were the great principles of Anglican reformation. It may be that they involved, as a consequence, increased liberty of conscience, and that, no doubt, followed upon them. Afterwards, the Rebellion and the Commonwealth asserted liberty of conscience for every one *except for the Church itself*, and the Revolu-

---

* The true Biblical and primitive belief in the Kingdom of Christ seems the proper antidote of the doctrine of Papal supremacy, and of its extreme opposite—the independent, isolating spirit of modern ultra-spiritualism. The Church has seemed so little to fulfil the hopes formed of a present reign of Christ, that men have looked forward to that reign as something future—either in a millennium on earth or an eternity in heaven. It is, however, undoubted, that the New Testament preached the Kingdom of Christ as close at hand when Christ came on earth, and as to be spread abroad when He ascended to His throne in heaven. It is indeed a militant Kingdom now, to be advanced by spiritual conquest continually, and only at last to be triumphant. But the reign of the Mediator is signally *now.* ' He must reign,' not after, but ' *until* He hath put all enemies under His feet' (1 Cor. xv. 25). And the reign, which is to follow that subjugation of the enemies, is not called the kingdom of Christ, but rather the reign when all shall be subject to Him that put all things under the Messiah, that then God may be all in all (1 Cor. xv. 28). Christianity, therefore, if it be all that it should be, is a living faith in the *personal* reign of a *present* King. Such a *present* King needs no viceroy, but should be surrounded and waited on by an united body of obedient subjects.

tion brought in the principle of general toleration, which was really a national rather than an ecclesiastical principle. But the great principles of the Reformation were the supremacy of Christ, the authority of Scripture, the return to primitive usages, and the independence of national Churches. Other things followed immediately from these. One was, that the quarrel between the *Regale* and the *Pontificale* was settled in favour of the former. It was no new principle that the King, and not the Pope, should be the ultimate appeal in ecclesiastical trials. That principle was enunciated at the time of Henry II. by the prelates and nobles in the Constitutions of Clarendon, which forbade appeals to be taken beyond the King's Court except by the King's consent, and which enacted that bishops should not be, like so many foreign princes, dependent only on the Pope, but should be barons of England, and do homage for their baronies to the King. The same principle was confirmed by Statute in the reign of Richard II. (16 Rich. II. ch. 5), and its maintenance had been constantly struggled for by every king that was strong enough to oppose the Pope. It was settled in the reigns of Henry VIII. and Elizabeth ; and, in fact, sprang directly from the principles (1) that there was no king but Christ, (2) that each national Church had independent rights, (3) that the Church consisted, not of the clergy only, but of the clergy and laity (or, in legal phrase, of the spiritualty and temporalty) of the land, united under the supreme power of that land —that supreme power, like every other, owing chief fealty and allegiance to Christ alone.

In a certain sense, then, the Reformation was the establishment of the Church, as at present understood.

Long before the Reformation, the Norman kings had, from time to time, asserted rights derived from their Saxon predecessors, viz. to be the chief governors of the whole realm, to govern the clergy as well as the laity, and to hear appeals in ecclesiastical as well as in civil causes. But the Reformation fully established these rights, and the submission of the clergy gave a further power to the Sovereign to restrain the promulgation of new canons without his authority and the consent of Parliament. Still, the real establishment of the Church, as well as its endowment, dates from the first acceptance of the Kingdom of Christ by the kingdoms of the Saxon Heptarchy, as elsewhere by the rest of the kingdoms of this world. And I cannot in any way escape the conviction that the disestablishing of the Church by any nation is the rejection by that nation of the Kingdom of our God and of His Christ. It is on this ground that I dread it—not for that Kingdom which shall never be destroyed, but for the kingdom and nation which, in refusing to serve the higher Kingdom, may, for that very refusal, perish.

In looking at Holy Scripture I seem to see two lines of promise, which run on, at first sight, without any apparent point of contact. The one is, that nations shall accept the Theocracy and be blessed by it—which has now been fulfilled for nearly fifteen centuries in Europe ; the other is, that the Theocracy, small as a grain of mustard-seed, shall grow larger and larger till it fills the earth ; but its growth is described as like that of a stone swelling up into a mountain, and at length falling upon the divided kingdoms of the world and breaking them to pieces (Dan. ii. 34, 35, 44). May it be that this first line has well-nigh run its course?

The Theocracy has been accepted by the kingdoms, but everywhere there seems a restlessness, and a taking council among the rulers ' to break its bonds asunder and cast away its cords from them.' Then is it so, that the second line shall be seen, not to run parallel, but to succeed in natural order to the first line ? The stone, hewn without hands, has been steadily growing, and is now a mountain. Is it to fall upon the nations which have rejected it, and to grind them to powder?

I cannot expect to make statesmen see these prophesies as I see them, but I fully believe that this is the course of events now to be expected. It appears to me that natural causes are all operating to produce exactly that which I read of in the Scriptures ; and the fulfilment in strictest detail of one line of prophecy confirms my anticipation and conviction that the other line will be fulfilled also.

And I do feel the greatest apprehension and the deepest sorrow, that my own country, which, more than any other country perhaps in Christendom, has accepted the Divine Kingdom and incorporated it into the very essence of its own kingdom, should be the first nation in Europe calmly, deliberately, and constitutionally, to disentangle itself, in an integral portion of its being, from that in the light of which only can men or nations hope to see light. It does not lessen, but increases the fear and the sorrow, to know and acknowledge that those who are now playing the first scene in this great tragedy are able and honest and good men, whom I have long honoured and esteemed. For the true and final prosperity of the Church itself I have not the slightest fear. Its natural heritage is labour and conflict and suffering ; but it must finally triumph. Possibly its danger of earthly desolation may give hope and promise of a higher and better comfort. Its children may gather more fondly round it, may forget their mutual jealousies in their common danger. And it will then be found that what the builders refused has indeed been the head stone of the corner. But if that which has been decreed in Ireland should, as so many hope and so many fear, be done in England too, it does seem to me, that whatever becomes of the Church, the prospect is very dreary for the land.*

* Probably very many desire the disestablishment of the Irish Church, the position of which all must admit to be anomalous, who yet do not desire the same for the English Church. Most people, however, now perceive that the one is at least very likely to draw after it the other. There is first a principle admitted never before known to our constitution. Then, if Ireland and Great Britain continue one nation, we shall have the three kingdoms with three different forms (or absence of forms) of faith ; the Parliament of which three kingdoms will legislate for the Church of the one kingdom of England. What likelihood is there that the Reformed Episcopal Church of England will be able to work under the guidance of a Parliament, one part out of three in which represents a Presbyterian nation, whilst another part represents either a Roman Catholic nation or a nation with no acknowledged faith ? Lastly, Scotland has long been drifting towards a state of opinion adverse to Church establishment ; Ireland, in its Protestant as much as in its Roman Catholic population, will in future be against the establishment of the English Church (and indeed against England altogether—so common report asserts) ; there will be added to these the dissenting party in England, and those members of the English Church who fret at what they believe to be State restraint. Thus, though the English Church is working zealously among an immense majority of the English people ; and though, probably, no national Church in Christendom is really more enshrined in the hearts of its members than the Church of England ; yet the force of circumstances seems almost certain, unless the Union be repealed, to carry the Church of England into the same gulf with the Church of Ireland.

At present the religion and the Church of Christ are interwoven into our national life and our national action, imperceptibly, but with a power which can scarcely be over estimated. Now, too, every village church, school, and parsonage forms a centre of civilization and Christianity in every corner and nook of England. Possibly voluntary gatherings may yet support a clergy in our towns; but what human probability is there that an educated gentleman will be maintained in our villages? Doubtless some agency, missionary, if not fixed, will be found to deal with these rural difficulties. But two things will almost infallibly result. One, that the clergy will steadily decline in social position and intellectual culture, and so in liberality of thought and life; the other, that they will aim at and attain to more of that so much talked of and so much dreaded priestly power, which seems the natural counterpoise of their otherwise more dependent position. In all human probability the nation will grow less religious in its national and family life, the clergy will grow less educated and less independent, and yet, as is the case in Roman Catholic countries, and among many dissenting bodies, more powerful in the direction of what is familiarly known by the name of priestcraft. This much, at least, appears to be inevitable. But the extent of the revolution which unsettles the Constitution of thirteen centuries must be far greater than this. It is not possible that the rest of the Constitution can stand, when the key-stone of its arch is gone. Many of those who now march in the thick and rapidly moving ranks of progress, know and feel that the progress will carry them far beyond their present views and their present hopes. Constitutional Monarchy, Hereditary Chambers, Constitutional Assemblies, and Parliamentary Government itself, will all be in imminent danger. There is only one thing which will not go, and that is the Theocracy. It may change its form, may be depressed, persecuted, for a time forgotten; but it cannot be stamped out, except by stamping out the life of the nation in which it reigns. Never but once was it stamped out by a people. The Jewish people, who had had it for fifteen centuries, stamped it out when they rejected its visibly - present King. That nation has never revived from the ruin which instantly overwhelmed it; but the Theocracy has gone on spreading and widening, and it now fills a larger area, and embraces a larger empire, than any empire—material, intellectual, or spiritual—which the world has ever known.

Of course I shall be told that these are the narrow views natural to a clergyman; though you will not tell me so. But in reply I say, that I do not think thus because I am a clergyman; but that I am a clergyman because I have thought thus with my earliest and deepest thoughts. It was because I believed in the Kingdom of Christ, and in the duty of every subject of that Kingdom to maintain and to advance it, that I sought to be a special minister under its King. If that Kingdom be not true, and that duty not paramount, then I willingly admit that all my life has been a delusion and a dream.

I have spoken of the dangers to the nation; I will say a very few words on the probable dangers to the faith, if the Church of England should, as most people expect, share, at no distant period, the fate of the Church of Ireland. There have been two great dis-

ruptions in Christendom ; one the division of the East
and West, the other the separation of the Reformed
Churches from Rome. The first was effected by the
great Eastern Patriarchs asserting their ancient equality
with, and independence of, the Roman Patriarch ; the
second was maintained chiefly by evoking the spirit
of nationality, and by asserting the independence of
national Churches. The so-called disestablishment of
a Reformed Church will be the reversal and abandonment of this latter principle. That principle was,
perhaps, at times too strongly asserted—so that reformers scarcely escaped the reproach of time-serving,
and nationality glided into Erastianism.* But its entire
abandonment will involve the loss of that which alone
has hitherto enabled individual Churches to maintain
their own independence. What will be the result ? It
is a happy dream of some, that faith may exist and
work in the world by its own force and goodness, and
with no united and organic action. But the dream will
soon be dispelled if ever we awake and find ourselves
Churchless. Such mere sporadic action neither accords
with Divine ordinance nor with earthly wisdom. Divine
ordinance points to a Theocratic Kingdom, ordered in
all things and sure. Earthly experience shows that
mere isolated effort works well for a time, and leaves

* Whether nationalism be a sound principle or not, it is wholly distinct from Erastianism. I have tried to show that nationalism is the
accepting by a nation of the Kingdom of Christ, and the mingling
of the life of that nation with the life of the Theocracy. Erastianism,
which is its counterfeit (*Diabolus simia Dei*), is the making religion
a mere department of the State ; not the support and defence of the
Church by the State, but the subjugation of the Church to the
State ; and the using of religion as a mere piece of State policy and
police administration.

D

no lasting fruit behind it. If the Churches of Great Britain and Ireland cease to be national, still their sphere of influence has spread so far and wide, that, by good and steady organization, the whole Anglican communion may perhaps be kept, as one great Patriarchate, united and independent. It cannot be done if every private opinion and every sectarian prejudice be pressed against the common good and to the disunion of the whole. But if clergy and laity will join together with mutual confidence, if men will fight and pray against extreme practices, against personal whims, against isolated and insubordinate courses, if they will renounce bitter recriminations, and, above all, discredit and discountenance violent religious periodicals (on the one side or the other), there may be a hope that united Anglicanism — at home, in America, and in the colonies — may hold fast to Catholic, primitive, and Evangelical truth, though its nationalism may have been scattered to the winds of heaven. *Otherwise, there is no hope but of re-absorption in Rome.* The danger of this latter alternative cannot be small, when so eminent a Protestant statesman as M. Guizot has contemplated it as very like to be necessary, if we are to dam-out the torrent of flood-tide infidelity. Union is vital to Christianity now ; and if Rome alone in Western Christendom exhibits an united front, it will draw a much larger host of earnest hearts into it than it has ever drawn yet. What will follow then it is impossible to speculate. The light of the Theocracy may grow fainter, and its glory more dim. Its subjects may suffer, may err, may sin. All we can be sure of is, that it will survive, as it has ever done ; and that at last it will triumph ; though over what ruins no wisdom can forecast.

And now I will relieve you of this long letter with an apology for its length, and with an earnest hope that, if I have written what I believe to be true, I have said nothing which you will feel to be offensive, or which will give you pain.

I remain, my dear Lord,

Ever, with the highest consideration and esteem,

Your Lordship's very faithful servant,

E. H. ELY.

LONDON: PRINTED BY
SPOTTISWOODE AND CO., NEW-STREET SQUARE
AND PARLIAMENT STREET

www.ingramcontent.com/pod-product-compliance
Lightning Source LLC
Chambersburg PA
CBHW032136080426
42733CB00008B/1099